My Life As A Tree

Gina Concialdi

To my husband, Mario, and my son, Sammy, you are the motivation and inspiration behind everything that I do.

To my mom, Pat White, thank you for always being supportive of my talents.

To my beautiful niece, Courtney Bowe, for her positive feedback and editing skills.

As I grow strong, my feet take hold,
circles around me as I grow old.

I stretch my arms and clap my hands, the wind blows through as nature demands.

Invited guest just rest and sing,
their favorite time is in the spring.

I hold the children
that frolic and play.

I am shelter for the animals that get away.

I carry messages from town to town,
upon my trunk wires are found.

I can grow fruit delicious and sweet,
I can grow nuts and berries to eat.

When it's time to be cut down, don't you worry, I'll be around.

I will sail the ocean from stem to stern, when I'm made into a boat with the money I've earned.

I will play beautiful music when I'm made into a cello, I will be standing next to a talented fellow.

Beautiful Music

I will slide you down the steepest hill, swishing and swaying with precision and skill.

I will provide you with paper and money to spend. I can even be an envelope or postcard to send.

I will shelter all who believe in me,
a lot of work for just one tree.

My story is the gifts
that I share with the world.
What will YOU share with the world?

I promise to live my life
Like the strongest tree
And explore all the gifts
INSIDE of ME.

The author and Illustrator, Gina Concialdi, is a Chicago native and has been an artist
since she was a child. She began taking art lessons from a neighborhood artist
and was painting in oils by age 14. As technology changed at a rapid pace,
she returned to college for the second time at age 50 with the help from Work-Net Illinois
and their WIOA education grant. She graduated with honors in 2018. She is an extrovert
with a sparkling personality that rubs off on everyone she meets. Her love of children,
books, nature, poetry and the contribution they return to the world, is what led
her to write this fun and colorful book.

"The Life Of A Tree" is a book about teaching children to see things in more
than one way. To teach them not to judge a book by its cover, but to look deeper to
discover more than what they see. This skill is paramount in building relationships
in life as well as creating an awareness of our natural resources and what they provide.
This book has profound message that will ignite the mind of any child as their
imagination expands and new questions are investigated.

www.ingramcontent.com/pod-product-compliance
Lightning Source LLC
Chambersburg PA
CBHW060812290526
45792CB00005BA/1620